Clara Barton

ANGEL OF THE BATTLEFIELD

Clara Barton

ANGEL OF THE BATTLEFIELD

by Rae Bains
illustrated by Jean Meyer

Troll Associates

Library of Congress Cataloging in Publication Data

Bains, Rae.
   Clara Barton, Angel of the Battlefield.

   Summary: A childhood biography of the girl who
became known as a fearless battlefield nurse
during the Civil War and the founder of the
American Red Cross.
   1. Barton, Clara, 1821-1912—Juvenile literature.
2. Nurses—United States—Biography—Juvenile
literature. [1. Barton, Clara, 1821-1912.
2. Nurses] I. Meyer, Jean, ill. II. Title.
HV569.B3B35   361.7'63 [B] [92]   81-23123
ISBN 0-89375-752-7   AACR2
ISBN 0-89375-753-5 (pbk.)

Clara Barton

ANGEL OF THE BATTLEFIELD

Christmas was always a happy time in the Barton house. But December 25, 1821 was an especially wonderful day. That was because this bright Christmas morning saw the birth of a healthy baby girl to Sarah and Stephen Barton.

The infant was washed and wrapped in a warm blanket. Then Captain Barton called his four other children into the bedroom to see their newborn sister. Seventeen-year-old Dorothy hurried in. She leaned over the cradle and smiled. Stephen, fifteen years old, and David, thirteen, joined her. And then in marched ten-year-old Sally, delighted not to be the family baby anymore.

Clarissa Harlowe Barton, the newborn's full name, brought endless joy to everyone. She was a sweet, calm baby who almost never cried. She was also a very smart little girl. This pleased her brothers and sisters. Baby Clara was their pet, and they gave her lots of love and attention.

Dorothy, a teacher at a local school, started her baby sister on the ABC's when she was only two years old. Clara was a good pupil, and she was reading by the time she was three. Sally did her share, too, teaching Clara to spell and to write.

Stephen taught his little sister arithmetic. Before she even started school, Clara could do simple addition, subtraction, multiplication, and division.

David taught her something very different. As Clara wrote years later, "He was the Buffalo Bill of the surrounding country....It was David's delight to...throw me upon the back of one colt, and spring upon another himself. Then he bid me to cling fast to the mane, and we galloped away....They were merry rides we took."

Clara was also her father's little pupil. He would sit her on his knee and tell her all about his battles as a soldier in the Indian Wars. Together, they studied maps. They traced the battle lines of the army's fierce encounter with the great warrior chief, Tecumseh. Mr. Barton taught Clara all of the military ranks, from private through general.

Only Mrs. Barton did not play teacher. "My mother," Clara remembered, "like the sensible woman that she was, seemed to conclude that there were plenty of instructors without her. She attempted very little...and looked on the whole thing with a kind of amused curiosity to see what they would make of me. Indeed, I heard her remark many years after that I came out of it with a more level head than she would have thought possible."

Even Button, the family dog, took special care of Clara. From the moment she was born, she was followed around by the white-haired, black-eyed animal. If Clara fell, Button tried to pick her up. If she dirtied her face and hands, he licked them clean. Every day, wherever she went, he went. Then, at night, when Clara knelt by her bed to say her prayers, Button sat beside her. And when she got into bed, Button would jump onto the covers and curl up at her feet. There he stayed until morning, her protector and friend.

Except for Sundays at church, Clara's first years were spent at home with her family. She had no other children to play with. Still, she wasn't unhappy. She had books to read, lessons to learn, horses to ride, and fields to run in with Button. Best of all, there were the six big people who loved her so much.

Then, when she was four, Stephen lifted her onto his shoulders and carried her through the snowdrifts to Colonel Richard Stone's school. It was the first day of winter term, and Clara's first day at school.

In the early 1800s, school was made up of two terms. Each term lasted three months. There was a winter term and a summer term. Spring and fall were important farming seasons. Most youngsters had to help with the planting in the spring, and the harvesting in the fall. So they didn't go to school then. Only the youngest pupils went to school in spring and fall.

Stephen kissed and hugged Clara, and said, "Be a good girl. I'll see you when school lets out." And he left.

Clara didn't know any of the other children. And she didn't know how to make friends. She was also much younger and smaller than any of the others. Some of the students—the ones who sat in the big seats in back—were teenagers. Even among the younger children, there was nobody younger than six years old. For the first time in her life, Clara felt scared and alone.

Colonel Stone rapped for attention on his desk. All talking stopped. He gave the bigger students arithmetic problems to do on their slates. Then he called the little ones to his desk. Holding up a spelling book with the alphabet in it, he began to point out the letters. As he said them out loud, Clara said them along with him.

"I named them all," Clara wrote years later. "Then I was asked to spell some little words, 'dog,' 'cat,' and so on."

Clara spelled them all correctly. Then she politely told Colonel Stone that she could spell even harder words. He tested her, and Clara did very well.

Colonel Stone told her to sit with the bigger
children. Clara was proud to be with the better
readers. She had no trouble keeping up with
them. But she continued to be lonely. When it
was play-time, the big children paid no attention
to her. And the little children, not knowing how
to act with this different girl, did not welcome
her into their groups.

Clara put every bit of her energy into learning. Geography became her new favorite subject when Colonel Stone gave her an atlas. She kept it with her day and night, reading it every chance she got.

Clara's interest in geography would be very important to her when she grew up. Clara always felt travel was easy and natural. She could picture, in her mind, the map of any place she was going to visit. New places never seemed strange to her, even if they were in another country. That was because she knew so many facts about them.

During the Civil War, when she was a battlefield nurse, Clara's knowledge of geography was of great help. She had no trouble reading military maps and memorizing them. She was never afraid of getting lost, and she could find any outpost, no matter where it was. This made it possible for her to bring aid to wounded soldiers quickly. Many lives were saved, thanks to Clara's childhood love of geography.

Life wasn't all school and study for Clara. She was also an active child, ready for any new game or adventure. And her brothers were always ready to take her out to play. One winter Sunday, long before dawn, Clara heard someone whistling under her bedroom window. She looked out, saw Stephen and David, and threw open the window.

"Dress warmly and come down," David whispered. "We're taking you skating."

"But I don't know how," Clara said.

"We'll teach you," Stephen said. "Hurry up. We'll wait here."

Clara rushed to dress and join her brothers. Then they were off to the ice-covered pond. The boys tied skate runners to her boots and wrapped two long woolen scarves around her waist. They each held the end of a scarf, to keep Clara on her feet.

The twinkling stars began to fade as the sun rose. Clara's cheerful laughter was like a bell tinkling on the crisp morning air. The boys pulled her back and forth over the smooth ice. Then one of her skates caught in a crack, throwing Clara to the ice. When she looked at her knees, the right one was bruised and cut a little. But the left one was badly cut and bleeding steadily.

David and Stephen took the scarves off Clara's waist and wrapped them around her knees. Then they helped her back to the house.

"We're sure to be punished for hurting Clara," said David.

"You will not be punished for anything!" Clara told them. "No one will even know that we went skating. I will keep my knees bandaged and my mouth closed."

Clara's long dress hid her injured knees. And she walked very carefully all day long. Even so, her left knee hurt terribly, and it was hard not to limp. But she could not let the pain show. That would give away their secret!

As hard as she tried, it became clear the next day that something was wrong. So, Clara let her parents look at her right knee. Then she told them, "I tripped on the stairs yesterday."

Mrs. Barton put a proper bandage on the slightly injured right knee and told Clara to walk the stairs more slowly.

Now that her parents knew she had a bruised knee, Clara could limp about the house. But she thought it was funny that nobody noticed that she was limping on the wrong leg!

The left knee, still wrapped in the scarf, soon became infected. At last, Clara had to show it to her parents. They called in the doctor, who cleaned the wound and put on a fresh bandage. Before he left, the doctor told Captain Barton, "That was a hard case, but she stood it like a soldier." Then he gave Clara orders to rest the leg for three weeks.

To make it easier for Clara to sit still for three long weeks, the Bartons gave her a copy of *The Arabian Nights.* It was a big book, filled with marvelous stories and beautiful pictures, and Clara loved it. Many years later, she remembered this book as one of her favorites.

But Clara felt very guilty. She could not eat or sleep. She knew she should be punished for hiding the truth about her accident, and for causing her parents such trouble and worry. Finally, her mother, seeing that something was bothering Clara, asked what it was.

Clara confessed all. Then, as she remembered years later, "My mother came to the rescue, telling me soothingly that she did not think it the worst thing that could have been done, and that other little girls had probably done as badly."

Mrs. Barton told Clara how she had misbehaved herself, when she was a child. She had gone riding on an untamed horse, even after her father had forbidden it. She had been thrown off the horse and hurt. "I did not need to be taught that lesson twice," Mrs. Barton told Clara. "I did not disobey my parents after that. And I think you will learn the same lesson I did."

Mrs. Barton was right—Clara had learned her lesson. She also learned how it felt to be in pain and need medical care. She thought of this many times when she was an adult. As Nurse Barton and founder of the American Red Cross, she made the easing of pain and suffering her life's work.

In the winter of 1829, when Clara was eight, she went away to a boarding school in a nearby town. It was a high school, also run by Colonel Stone, and it was one of the best schools in that part of Massachusetts.

Clara's parents had two reasons for sending her to boarding school. It would give the extremely bright youngster the chance to study Latin, ancient history, and many other new subjects. They also hoped that living in a house with other children would help her overcome her great shyness.

Clara loved the schoolwork, and was one of Colonel Stone's top students. But being away from home didn't cure her shyness. It just made her homesick. She cried all the time, did not want to eat, and had little to do with the other children. Clara stayed there only one term. Then her father, Colonel Stone, and the Barton family doctor all agreed that Clara would be better off at home.

Her education did not stop. Her brothers and sisters again took over the job of teaching her. And Clara learned a lot more on her own. Early in 1830, the family moved into an old house that needed a great deal of work. Sylvanus Harris, a local painter and paperhanger, was hired to do the job. Clara watched him for hours, mixing colors, painting, and making his own putty and plaster.

Mr. Harris's work was so interesting that Clara wanted to try it, too. So, in a timid voice, she asked him, "Will you teach me to paint, sir?"

"With pleasure, little lady," he said. "If your mamma is willing, I should very much like your help."

Mrs. Barton gave her permission. The next morning, dressed in an old smock, the little girl reported to Mr. Harris. "I was taught how to hold my brushes," Clara wrote, "to take care of them, allowed to mix and blend my paints, and shown how to make putty and use it."

Clara worked with Mr. Harris day after day. She enjoyed every minute of it. And when the work was done after a month, she was very proud of herself and pleased to have learned so much. But she was also sad that there was no more to do.

The last night of Mr. Harris's job, when Clara went to her room, she found a box on her candle stand. In it was a tiny locket, engraved with the words: "To a Faithful Worker." Clara kept that locket all her life.

She also kept the skills she had gained. As an adult, she did her own painting and wallpapering wherever she lived. As she liked to point out, "People should not say that this or that is not worth learning, giving as their reason that it will not be put to use. They can no more know what information they will need in the future than they will know the weather two hundred years from today."

When she was eleven, Clara had to take time off from her schoolwork. Her brother David had been seriously hurt falling off a barn roof. It took two years for him to recover. And Clara was his devoted nurse for those two years.

Once David was on his feet again, he taught Clara a number of skills he felt were important. She learned to drive a nail properly and to use a hammer and saw. She learned to throw a ball far and accurately and to tie sturdy square knots. Most important, David taught her how to plan her work carefully, and how to do a good job from start to finish. Clara, as always, was an "A" student.

As soon as David was completely recovered, Clara returned to school. She studied grammar, English literature, composition, history, philosophy, chemistry, and writing. Her parents were pleased with her high grades, but worried that she was still terribly shy. They wondered what her future would be if she stayed this way.

When Clara was fifteen, a guest at the Barton home made an interesting prediction about Clara's future. He was L. N. Fowler, an expert in the field of phrenology.

Phrenology was a popular "science" of the time. Phrenologists believed there were thirty-seven small sections in the human head. Each of these sections controlled something about a person. There were sections for size, weight, hope, humor, secretiveness, and so on. Phrenologists also believed they could "read" a person's character by reading the bumps on the head.

Mr. Fowler felt Clara's head and said, "The sensitive nature will always remain. She will never assert herself for herself. But for others she will be perfectly fearless. Throw responsibility upon her. She has all the qualities of a teacher. As soon as her age will permit, give her a school to teach."

42

Perhaps after hearing Mr. Fowler's words, Clara began to gain courage and faith in herself. If he said she had the strength to be a teacher, why then, that's just what she would be! And so, the girl who was too shy to speak up when she was a student, became a teacher in charge of forty children. She was only seventeen. Some of her students were almost as old as she, and a few were bigger than their small, slim teacher. But that didn't scare her.

The biggest pupils were four teenage boys. Clara was warned that they had bullied last year's teacher. On Clara's first day as their teacher, she set out to prove that she was in charge. All morning Clara kept firm control of the class, while the teenage boys watched her for signs of weakness. Then came recess.

Outside, the class began to play ball. Clara asked if she could get in the game. This was just the kind of thing the four boys were waiting for. Now they'd make her look foolish in front of everybody.

But Clara—who had learned to play ball well
—surprised them. Very quickly, the boys saw
that Clara was a fine athlete. She was strong
and could run fast. She could throw a ball as
straight and as far as any of them. The boys
soon had a deep respect for their young teacher.

Clara never had a bit of trouble from those
boys—or anyone else—at the school.

Her career as a teacher continued until 1853. During that time, she taught at several schools in Massachusetts and New Jersey. Then, in 1854, she moved to Washington, D.C., where she became the first female clerk in the United States Patent Office. But it wasn't until the bloody Civil War began that Clara Barton began her greatest service. Learning of the needs of the soldiers, she plunged herself into serving those needs. She had no title or help from the government. She was simply doing what she felt was right.

From the start, no task was too hard for Clara to undertake. Still too shy to speak up for herself, she made speeches to large groups, begging for money to buy bandages, medicine, food, clothing, soap, towels—anything and everything the soldiers needed.

As the war went on, Clara Barton became a living legend. She was called the "Angel of the Battlefield," nursing Union and Confederate soldiers with equal love and attention.

After the Civil War ended, Clara traveled to Europe. There, she was honored by many governments for her bravery and goodness. And it was there that she learned of a new organization called the Red Cross. The aim of the Red Cross was to help people in need, in war and peace. Its flag—a red cross on a field of white—told everyone that help was at hand.

Clara returned to the United States, determined to make the Red Cross a symbol of help and mercy throughout her own nation. She spent the rest of her long life doing just that, bringing aid wherever fire, flood, or any other form of disaster struck. When Clara Barton died at the age of 90, the Red Cross had become a permanent part of American life.